For "Muscamigo"
Oct 14, 1994   Age 7

FUNDAMENTALS OF FREE LUNGEING

FUNDAMENTALS OF FREE LUNGEING

Stephen A. Mackenzie, Ph.D.
Foreword by Dr. James P. McCall

Half Halt Press, Inc.
Boonsboro, Maryland

Fundamentals of Free Lungeing:
An Introduction to Tackless Training

© Stephen A. Mackenzie

Published in the United States of America

Half Halt Press, Inc.
P.O. Box 67
Boonsboro, MD 21713

Designed by Jim Haynes, Graphics Plus

Illustrations by Laurie Mackenzie

Photographs by Denise Grexer

Library of Congress Cataloging-in-Publication Data

Mackenzie, Stephen Alexander.
    Fundamentals of Free Lungeing / by Stephen A. Mackenzie;
Illustrations by Laurie Mackenzie; photos by Denise Grexer.
        p.   cm.
    ISBN 0-939481-35-9
    1. Lungeing (Horsemanship) I. Title
SF287.M145   1994
636.1'088–dc20

DEDICATION

*To my wife Laurie,
who introduced me to tackless training
and then helped and supported me
in my quest to understand it.*

TABLE OF CONTENTS

Chapter: **Page**

Foreword Ho! Dr. James P. McCall *11*

Chapter 1 – Advantages *13*

Chapter 2 – Necessary Facilities and Equipment *17*

Chapter 3 – The Behavioral Basis *23*

Chapter 4 – Starting, Stopping and the Balance Point........... *35*

Chapter 5 – The Outside Turn....................................... *49*

Chapter 6 – The Inside Turn.. *59*

Chapter 7 – Backing up *69*

Chapter 8 – Calling Your Horse to You *77*

Chapter 9 – Submission Training *85*

Chapter 10 – Confidence Building *89*

Chapter 11 – Priorities *93*

Chapter 12 – Beyond the Basics *97*

◆

ACKNOWLEDGMENTS

This book describes techniques which were invented and perfected by Dr. James P. McCall and his wife Lynda, who pioneered the concept of tackless training before it became popular. All of us who use or teach this style of training are deeply indebted to them.

This book exists primarily because of the students in the horse program at the State University of New York at Cobleskill. Their required course involving free lungeing had no written material to support their efforts in the round pen. Their constant complaints about the lack of written material and demands that something be done about it finally motivated the author to devise a systematic description of McCall-style free lungeing and an equally systematic explanation of why it works.

Acknowledgment should also be given to Nelson, a grey Quarter Horse gelding who graciously served as the model in the photographs.

◆

Foreword Ho!

F or as long as I can remember, I have been a student of body language communication. To me, this is not a highly specialized field within some academic discipline but an adventure into a form of communication that underlines the exchange of information between two individuals regardless of their species. I also believe that I am not one of a few scientists working to unravel the subconscious messages in body language but a member of the human race, and all of us are striving, either subconsciously or consciously, to decipher the messages delivered by expressions.

Within our species this task is aided by our highly developed verbal skills which can be expressed by the spoken word or transcribed into written language. Other animals are not so gifted and their communication relies most heavily on body language. Therefore, to communicate most effectively with a member of another species, we need to be able to give and receive information using their intrinsic language. This is the basis of my philosophy of horse training and Steve Mackenzie's discussions on this subject are direct and to the point, explaining how important this skill is for trainers and owners of horses in their interactions. His observations on how to talk horse are punctuated by relevant and humorous anecdotes that the author has experienced through many years of using and teaching free lungeing techniques to horse people and horses; for one's level of expertise in free lungeing is directly correlated to his understanding of horse body language. And personal space.

Steve's explanation of this concept of personal space is one of the clearest I have read. His creative descriptions of different types of human body positions and what they mean to the horse should be read by everyone involved with horses. But don't quit there.

All animal trainers are aware of the individual differences which exist within each individual and it is the ability to handle these differences that sets the great trainers apart from the barely-a-horse trainers. Steve's in-depth discussion of the formation of the balance point between horse and human and how this point must be adjusted for each horse provides a strong case for individuality. Since this balance point is like the gearshift in a standard transmission automobile, one cannot control the movement or direction of the horse without understanding where the "gear" is located and how to get from one "gear" to another.

To try and bring the important of individuality home, Steve has devoted an entire chapter to an analysis of two opposite personality types — the insecure and secure horse. It is this kind of attention to individual variation that allows free lungeing to work for horses of all breeds ranging from the most dominant to the most submissive member.

I think that horsemen at all levels of expertise will gain useful information from reading this book. For the person unfamiliar with the use of body language and its application in free lungeing, a new world will open up. They will be moving differently around their horse in and out of the lunge pen — a change that will lead to a more positive relationship.

For the horseman already familiar with the technique known as free lungeing, Steve's thoughtful analysis will provide fodder to move to a higher plane of understanding of the horse. As for myself, after having read the book, I appreciated the new and better words by which to interpret body language and I am proud to say Steven Mackenzie was my student.

CHAPTER 1

Advantages

T o many people, tackless training is an interesting toy which has no relevance to the real
world. This is unfortunate because they are
missing out on one of the most effective methods of improving their
horse-related skills. Free lungeing, when applied properly, offers the
horseman many advantages.

The first of these is the improvement of the human's ability to communicate. Free lungeing is highly dependent upon visual communication, which is the main form of communication between horses.
Unfortunately, many humans are sloppy with their body language and
expect the horse to focus on their vocal commands during early training. This teaches the horse to ignore our body cues and pay more
attention to the noises we make. It also encourages us to avoid precision in the way we handle horses. Lack of precision dooms us to a life
of mediocre relationships with our horses.

Good free lungeing, however, forces us to improve our body signals
right from the start. We soon become better at approaching horses in
the stall or field and have much less trouble working around horses in
general. This makes it a wonderful way to teach beginners. They
immediately start trying to think like a horse, instead of waiting for
some painful experience to motivate them.

Experienced students who prefer to wrestle physically with horses
instead of out thinking them also benefit from the technique. They
first find that they have no physical connection with the horse. After
feeling helpless for a brief time, they begin to realize that they must
master the horse with their mind, since there is nothing to grab and

fight with. Instructors will find this an invaluable tool, not just for their students, but for their own development as well. Paying more attention to our own body language encourages us to pay more attention to the horse's body signals as well. Regardless of present skill levels, this invariably leads to a human who can read horses better. Few things can improve a person's training or working ability more than that. Consequently, whether you are a beginner or a successful Olympic coach, good free lungeing can make you even better than you are.

Those of you who train young, inexperienced horses to accept riders or vehicles will find the green breaking process is much quicker when you use tackless methods. This makes them very time efficient and economical procedures for people who train for a living. Standard techniques require the horse to learn a system of communication which is not natural for him, leading to a certain amount of confusion. The end result is an increase in training time. Good free lunging is an imitation of the horse's own paralanguage which he already understands (a paralanguage is a language that is not as complete as the ones humans use). This cuts training time by a third and has an additional benefit. Horses exhibit less stressful body language when good free lungeing is taking place than is often seen with standard methods. It is possible that since there is less confusion, there is also less stress on the horses. Assuming, of course, that the trainer is doing it well.

Green breaking is not only faster when tackless methods are employed, it is also safer for horse and human. This is mainly due to the fact that it is easier to recognize when the horse is ready to comfortably accept a rider or cart. When the horse willingly gives us the leadership role and stops resisting us mentally, there is a noticeable change in the way he works for us in the training pen. Instead of us having to make the horse follow commands, the horse starts working cooperatively with us. Free lungeing becomes much like a dance performed by a skilled pair of dancers. The trainer leads and the horse follows with such smoothness and flow that the experience becomes almost addictive to some humans – particularly those unaccustomed to getting cooperation from their horses.

The difference in behavior is so noticeable that no talented person can miss it. When this change takes place, the horse is ready to accept anything from you provided you do it in a reasonable manner and don't frighten him. In other words, it is then time to begin introducing the cart or rider. As long as you don't frighten him, the horse will not resist you. This takes much of the guess work out of green breaking and allows a skillful person to drastically reduce the chances of injury to both horse and human, something that should make sense to all horsemen. If you are an amateur, you probably have a strong personal bond with your horse and wish to keep him healthy. You also need to stay healthy yourself for your other responsibilities in life. If you are an instructor, reducing the chances of injury is the best liability insurance you can buy. If you are a professional trainer, you don't make money by paying large veterinary bills and you certainly don't make money lying in a hospital bed. Choosing a technique which reduces the chances of injury is simply a good business decision.

You can also learn much about older, problem horses by free lungeing them. For some reason many horses, when at liberty in the training pen, feel free to express themselves differently than they do under tack or when connected to a lunge line. I suspect this has something to do with the fact that they know you can do things to them when there is a physical connection. At any rate, horses which seem perfectly well mannered when on a lunge line will often show you something different when loose. This can be the key to diagnosing their problems and solving them.

Problem horses can be quite different from each other and it is unlikely that any useful definition will fit them all. However, the root of many problems is the basic relationship between the horse and the humans in his life. If this relationship is improved, many of the problems we have as trainers disappear. Free lungeing is an extremely useful tool for this purpose. Certain procedures create mental pressure on horses and encourage dominant horses to think more submissively. Other procedures release mental pressure and encourage overly submissive or frightened horses to think and act more confidently. By balancing these techniques, a trainer can produce confident horses with just the desired degree of submission. Such horses rarely have major problems.

So whether you are an instructor, or trainer of green or experienced horses, free lungeing, or tackless training, have something to offer you. My students also claim that it is simply more fun working horses this way. And they are the experts on fun.

CHAPTER 2

Necessary Facilities and Equipment

F ree lungeing can be accomplished in many environments. Over the years I have worked successfully in indoor arenas, oval, rectangular and square paddocks, round pens and several different forms of temporary arena. The quality of my work, however, is dependent upon the facility to which I am assigned. If we exclude the mere chasing of horses by some person with a whip (which can be done in any enclosed area, takes no talent and should be considered exercising, not free lungeing), free lungeing is best conducted in a circular training arena, commonly called a round pen. Such an area allows us to keep more consistent contact with the horse and avoid disruptions of the process by the horse ducking into corners at inopportune times. While you can accomplish your goals in other types of arena, a round pen allows you to progress more quickly and smoothly. This in turn creates less stress for you and the horse.

While they vary considerably in detail, round pens that are well suited to free lungeing will have the following characteristics. They will be weather proof. In some locations this will mean roofs, wind breaks and heaters, while in others you may need shade and a breeze. They will be large enough in diameter to prevent undue stress on the legs of the horses worked in them (certain larger breeds may need larger diameters). They will have good, safe footing. They will be sturdy enough to prevent the horse from running through the wall or kicking holes in it. The walls will be tall enough to discourage horses from trying to jump out and they will not have gaps or holes large enough for a hoof to pass through. They will be free of sharp projections and the other numerous things that horses injure themselves on.

17

Those of you who have experience in round pens will probably have personal preferences about how to build them. By all means build them in such a way that you are comfortable working in them. Just be sure to include the characteristics listed in the above paragraph. If you have limited experience with them, you may not know how to have one constructed. To get you started, a schematic of the round pen here at SUNY Cobleskill is included *(see Figures 2.1 and 2.2)*

It may not be perfect for you, but it is a good starting point. With a few modifications you should be able to come up with something that will serve you well. If you still don't like it, there are some building companies that sell ready-made round pens, you may want to check them out. Our pen is a modification of one I worked in at Dr. Jim McCall's and has stood the test of time. My students have successfully trained many a green horse in it. A draft horse tried to knock it down once (she did manage to shake it quite well) and light horses have tried to jump out of it, but all to no avail. Not only did it thwart them, but the horses were not injured. It is essentially an eight foot high circular wall with no gaps in it. It is 45 feet in diameter (this is the best size for teaching inexperienced human students) with one of the sections made hollow and hinged to swing inwards, acting as a door. The wall has a five degree outward slope to it, to prevent student's knees from contacting the wall when they are riding. This also allows gravity to close the door section and hold it shut. The door has a chain and hook to prevent high winds from blowing it open.

The chain was added after our only successful escape. One windy day a few years ago, a boarder horse in for training was working on the wall at the trot when a large gust of wind came up. This horse had not been handled before we received her (she had been herded onto the trailer to get her to us). While she was still hard to catch, I was just noting mentally that she was coming along nicely. Those of you familiar with Murphy's Law know exactly what happened next. As the horse was a few strides from the door, the gust of wind blew the door half way open, creating a perfect opening for a horse to fit through. Without so much as blinking an eye, the horse trotted through the opening, the wind died and gravity pulled the door closed. This left me with a hard-to-catch horse taking an unauthorized tour of campus and the student trainer standing in the center of the ring wondering

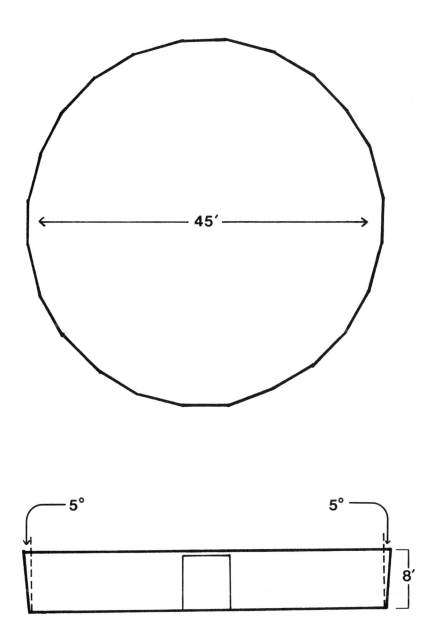

Figure 2.1. Schematic of the round pen at SUNY Cobleskill showing the basic dimensions, slant of the walls to protect the knees of riders, and the door.

Figure 2.2. The round pen at SUNY Cobleskill showing the door
(last wall section on the left) and the stairs leading up to the
observation deck.

where her horse went. The horse never even broke stride or hesitated. The chain went on the door the next day.

Many people do good work in pens of different dimensions and I am not saying that your pen has to be like ours. For instance, if I were purely a horse trainer instead of an instructor, I might want a pen 60 feet in diameter instead of 45 feet (which is best for humans to learn in). The above information is offered only as a suggestion to get some of you started

Once you have a functional facility, you need some way to punish the horse from a safe distance. This is kept to a minimum, but cannot be completely avoided in most cases. Free lungeing is actually an imitation of the way an equine herd leader handles other members of the herd. There are times in the real world when the herd leader punishes inappropriate behavior and we need to be able to imitate that. Otherwise the horse will become confused and we will have unnecessary problems. We usually use a short driving whip for this purpose, not to abuse the horse, but to administer a simple whack at the time when the equine herd leader would probably be doing something far more violent. We have found that we do not have to match the actual level of violence shown by the equine leader in order to be effective, but we do need to act in the same general fashion. While other instruments could be used, the whip seems to be sufficient. If a horse has a tendency to kick, a longer whip is beneficial.

Time is another important tool. We normally work adult horses no more than fifteen minutes in the round pen. Their attention spans vary, of course, but fifteen minutes is a good upper limit to start with. As you gain experience with a particular horse, you can adjust accordingly.

CHAPTER 3

The Behavioral Basis

M ost systems of training are designed from the human's point of view. Consequently, they make sense to us but do not always follow principles which are natural for horses. This puts most of the burden on the less intelligent member of the partnership, which doesn't make sense. The style of tackless training described in this book differs considerably from this approach. When he decided to change his style of training, Dr. McCall started by observing horses interacting with each other. The idea was to identify how horses gain control of each other, since that would be the training method they would understand best. It would be a system of their own choosing, not ours. It should be less confusing to the horse, which should speed up the training process, and less stressful mentally. What developed was an imitation of the manner in which an equine leader works to obtain control of his herdmates and the use of cues that most closely resemble the actual signals used between horses. This puts the mental burden on the human, supposedly the more intelligent member of the partnership. While no training method is ever likely to be perfect, this approach makes a lot more sense than most.

It is no secret that horses have a pronounced interest in the space that immediately surrounds them *(see Figure 3.1)*. Control of this area is often linked to certain life styles, such as dominant horses using their space to run others off a food source. In some instances, this becomes a matter of life and death, when they interact with predators, for instance. Consequently, horses that seek control over other horses begin by trying to control the space around themselves. Once they have achieved that, they try to control the space around others.

If they can gain control of the space around another horse, they have effectively achieved control of the animal himself. Conversely, if a horse allows another horse to control his space without resistance, he is giving control to the other horse. This is why so much importance is placed on the act of "herding," since it signals the control of one animal over others.

Horses seem to have agreed amongst themselves that when higher ranking horses are giving "go away" signals, lower ranking animals should move out of their space, which serves to lower the amount of aggression or fighting in the herd. So if we can give "go away" signals and get a horse to move out of our space in the same manner, he will eventually start to think of us as a higher ranking animal. This is one of the keys to good free lungeing. By systematically herding the horse around, we are portraying ourselves as leaders and giving the horse a chance to express what he thinks about our leadership. As the horse yields more to our leadership, the lungeing becomes more fluid and graceful, until the horse yields completely to our herding. We can then move on to other matters with a willing, cooperative horse.

To herd properly, we need to know more about how horses communicate. While it is beyond the scope of this work to completely define the horse's paralanguage, a discussion of the signals used in free lungeing is in order.

Horses communicate using most of their senses, including sight, sound, touch and smell. In free lungeing, we imitate some of the visual cues, which seem to be the most important in herding. Since we are anatomically different, we will not be able to imitate them with complete accuracy, but the closer we can come, the easier it will be for the horse to understand us.

Let us divide the signals we find useful for free lungeing into four groups: distance increasing (or "go away"); distance decreasing (or "come here"); directional; and modifying.

Distance increasing ("go away") signals include:

1) Direct eye contact.

2) Orienting the body axis as though you are going to approach the horse (we can call this frontal body axis for short)

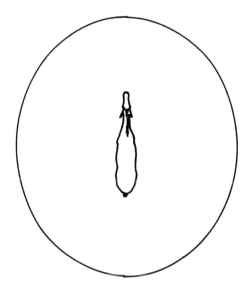

Figure 3.1. A horse and his space.

3) Movement of any sort towards the horse (this could be leaning, stepping or walking).

4) Fast limb movements (such as fast hand waving or short, fast, bouncy steps with the feet).

5) Stamping the feet on the ground.

The direct eye contact and frontal body axis can be seen in horses when a large number of them are turned out together and a dominant horse prepares to attack an offending herd member. If he has time and opportunity, he looks straight at the offender, turning his body axis to face the offender squarely so he can run straight forward to make contact. Then, any movement toward the other horse results in movement away from him by the offender.

The faster and more deliberate the approach, the stronger the signal to move away seems to be. If the offender does not move away, some form of violence results. Fast limb movements resemble striking motions, so it should not be surprising that horses move away from them like they would from any aggressive motion. Foot stomping can be seen in almost any annoyed or aggressive horse. It is a clear signal to increase space around it. When we want horses to move away from us, we should do our best to imitate these signals.

Distance decreasing ("come here") signals are often the opposite of the increasing signals. They include:

1) Breaking eye contact.

2) Turning the body axis slightly sideways.

3) Any movement away from the other animal.

4) Slow limb movements.

5) The absence of foot stomping.

Breaking direct eye contact signals a more sideways posture. This, and turning the body axis slightly sideways, is effective since it is the reverse of what you do to attack effectively. In other words, since horses cannot attack effectively sideways, this is a non-threatening posture to assume. Movement away from the horse draws him in your direction due to an age-old desire of most horses to maintain contact with the herd. When they were wild on the plain for instance, it was important not to be separated from the herd; those who were usually died at the hands of predators. Horses who were interested in maintaining the connection between their space and that of the next herd member tended to live longer and pass their genes on to the next generation. There has been little reason to actively breed such instincts out of domestic horses and so there are still many that seek to maintain the connection of their space with yours if you are the only two in the training pen. When you have a good connection with the horse, he will move towards you when you move back and threaten to break the connection. When we are trying catch or call our horses to us, we should imitate these signals.

Directional cues do not seek to directly affect the distance between the horse and trainer, but rather the direction the horse is inclined to move. They include:

> **1)** Projecting your space into a certain area, including projecting distance increasing signals at a particular area and stepping sideways to block forward movement.

> **2)** Shoulder and or hip twisting to indicate the desired direction of a maneuver.

Projecting space behind the horse using distance increasing signals is effective for the same reason that distance increasing signals are effective. It leaves only one respectful way for the horse to respond, the forward direction *(see figures 3.2, 3.3 and 3.4)*.

Shoulder twisting and blocking movement by stepping sideways can be seen when dominant horses are driving or herding. They also use their long necks, which is all we usually notice, but if you ignore the head and neck, you will see that they also use the shoulders and front feet. While we can't imitate the head and neck very well, we can substitute the shoulders, hips and feet for them. Horses respond quite well to this.

Modifying cues serve to back up the major cues listed above. They would include:

> **1)** Use of the arms to emphasize shoulder movements.

> **2)** Use of arms, hands and legs to apply pressure in places the major cues leave unaffected.

> **3)** Any other body movement that the horse reacts to.

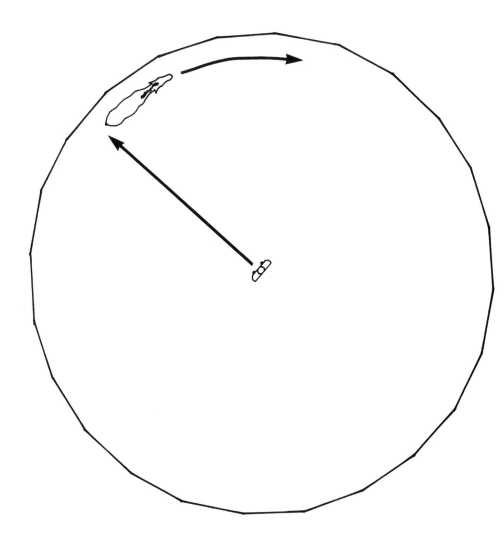

Figure 3.2. Human in the center of the ring giving distance increasing signals to the rear of the horse, which respectfully moves forward.

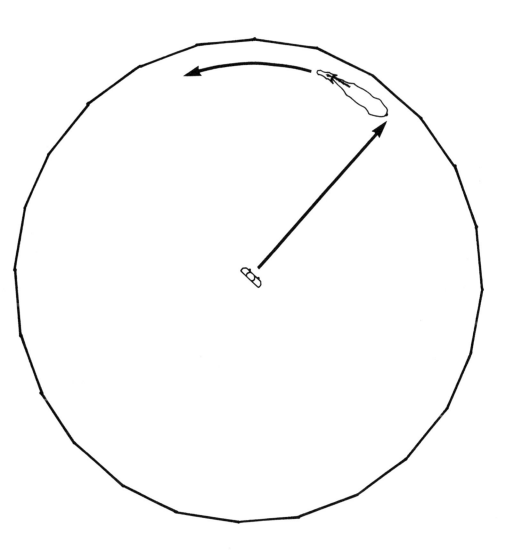

Figure 3.3. Same as Figure 3.2.

By combining the above cues in different ways, we can manipulate the space of a horse in such a way that we control his speed and direction of travel. We can do this so effectively that a talented human can get a confident, cooperative horse to start, stop, walk backwards, reverse direction away from the center of the ring (known as an outside turn), reverse direction towards the center of the ring (known as an inside turn), do circles in one half of the arena and even figure eights. The gait and speed of the horse can also be controlled so well that the horse will pick up whatever gait you wish at the exact point in the pen that you desire.

This all assumes that you have a cooperative horse. It is important to remember that free lungeing is not a magic wand that will make all horses behave instantly. What it will do is insure that the horse understands what you are telling him to do. At that point, the horse still has to decide whether or not to obey you.

A truly dominant horse will ignore your signals completely and even start signaling you back, expecting you to comply. A frightened horse may understand your signals but lack the confidence to carry them out. If your relationship with your horse is basically good but needs improving, he may obey some cues and ignore the rest. The trick in these cases is to motivate the horse to comply, which is discussed in later chapters. Tackless training is a marvelous tool for molding a horse's mind, but remember that there is a big difference between a horse *understanding* you and obeying you.

Many people get confused on how to reward or punish a horse during this type of tackless training. Rewards can be delivered in different ways. Since much of what we do involves the pressure of distance increasing signals, we can use the release of pressure to great effect. When the horse does something well, all we have to do is to step back slightly, stand still and lower our space by taking a deep breath and letting it all out as we let our shoulders and energy droop *(see figure 3.5)*.

Horses are very responsive to this form of reward, technically known as "negative reinforcement." It is unfortunate that scientists chose that name, since it suggests that something bad is happening. What it really means is that something is being removed from the horse and the horse likes the removal so much that he considers it a reward worth working for. Perhaps a better name would have been a "removal reward."

To give a bigger reward, we can remove pressure even further by using distance decreasing signals to call the horse into the center of the ring and into our space *(see chapter 8)*. Most horses seek herd acceptance and like to be invited into the leader's space, so this is a powerful reward. When the horse gets to you, you can administer all the positive reinforcement you like in the normal fashion, which adds to the power of the reward *(see figure 3.6)*. Naturally, you can use your voice to give secondary rewards at any time, but it is not usually necessary if you use the primary ones (pressure release and mutual grooming) properly. When you use your voice for a reward, remember that it is a secondary reward and must be properly paired with a primary reward many times in order to have maximum effect.

Punishments are given in standard ways. If you have a timid horse and you do not wish to frighten him, you can merely protest his actions by making an unpleasant noise or whistling the whip in the air. This would represent the weakest of punishments, but it is sufficient for some timid horses. To increase the level of severity, you can hit the ground with the whip. You can increase severity even farther by stepping towards the horse as you do so. If the horse has a normal level of confidence, it is often best to make physical contact at least once by whacking him with the whip. Horses know what a bluff is and that animals who make them are not really serious about hitting them. They will often take advantage of such individuals. If you make contact in the beginning of the workout, they know you are not bluffing and will often choose not to challenge you. This way you end up giving very few punishments and lots of rewards, which is what we would all like.

When giving a punishment, remember not to work against yourself. For example, if the horse has just ignored a cue to stop, don't punish him by running at the rear end of the horse and whacking him there. That will only make him run and increase the momentum, which was the problem in the first place. In such a case you should get out in front of the horse and whack him in the chest from the front, encouraging him not to go forward so fast next time. You must use good horse sense when applying rewards or punishments.

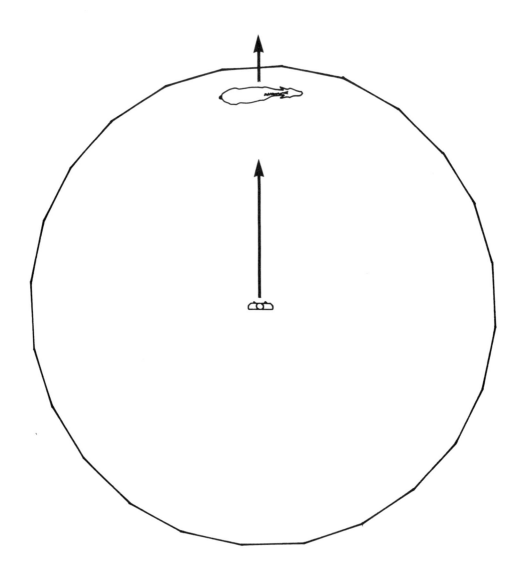

Figure 3.4. Human directing distance increasing signals improperly. With no free area to move respectfully into, many horses will go sideways to try to break the wall, or straight up in the air.

Figure 3.5. Author dropping his space and energy to reward a Quarter Horse gelding named "Nelson" for a nice stop.

Figure 3.6. Having called Nelson over to him, the author applies positive reinforcement in the form of mutual grooming.

CHAPTER 4

Starting, Stopping and the Balance Point

Once you and your horse are securely in the round pen, it pays to spend some time socializing before you start working. If horses think that you will begin driving them instantly every time you enter the pen, some will begin to run away from you without looking for what kind of signals you are giving. This may be fine for exercising, but it is not good for communication. So spend a minute or two stroking the horse's neck or giving him some sort of pleasant attention at the beginning of each session *(see figure 4.1)*. When the socializing is over, give the horse distance increasing signals to move him away from you and out towards the wall of the pen. Be sure that the rear end of the horse does not pass close to you as you do this. Some horses will kick up one or both hind feet as they move past you towards the wall. Have your whip ready and move the horse away from you, and do not let him walk past you to get to the wall.

Once he is on the wall, you have many options, one of which is to ask him to move forward. One way to do this is to move in towards the horse while giving distance increasing signals until you feel your spaces connect *(see figures 4.2 and 4.3)*. Sometimes your spaces will connect while you are standing in the center of the ring, in which case you don't need to move. You know you have connected when the horse moves in response to your movements, whether he shows only a muscle twitch, raises his head or actually walks. You can then use your directional cue of focusing your "go away" signals on the rear end of the horse. If the horse decides to be respectful, he will move forward to get out of your space.

Figure 4.1. The beginning of each training session should include some socialization between human and horse.

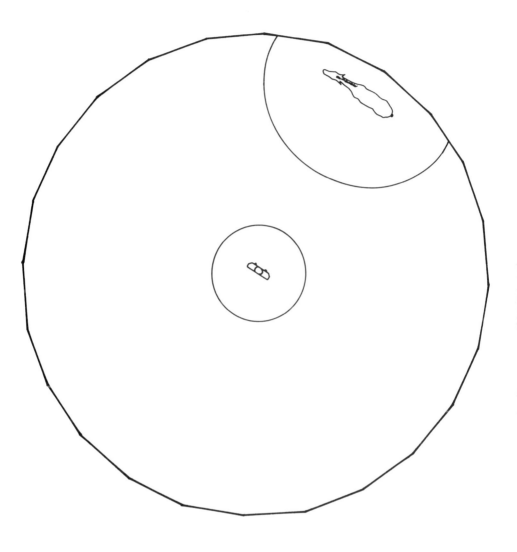

Figure 4.2. Human and horse with spaces not connected. The size of the spaces will vary between individuals.

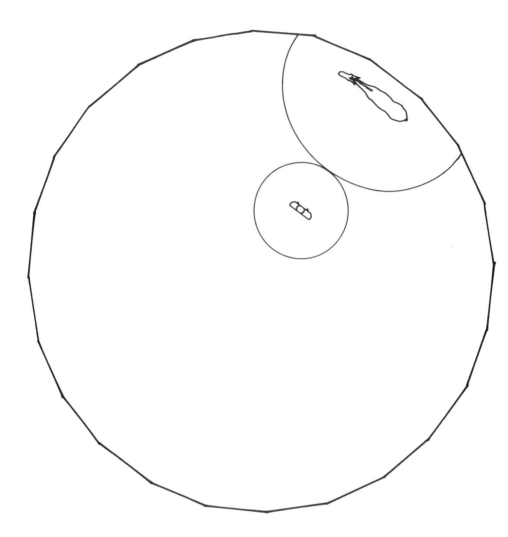

Figure 4.3. Spaces connected. In this case, the human had to move toward the horse to make the connection. When the human has a larger space, this is not necessary.

It is often helpful to think of the horse as a wet bar of soap that you are holding against the shower wall with one open hand. If you move your hand to one end of it and press against the wall, the soap will slip out away from the pressure of your hand. If you think of the pressure of your space as the hand, a respectful horse as the soap and the round pen wall as the shower wall, you will see many similar reactions. It is often helpful to use the hips and or shoulders to bump the rear end of the horse with your space and encourage him to go the correct direction *(see figure 4.4)*. While any of these components may work by themselves on certain horses, it has become standard to combine them all to ask a horse to move forward. So the standard cue to go forward has become:

1) Be sure your spaces are connected.

2) Direct distance increasing signals to the rear end of the horse.

3) Twist the rear shoulder and hip (nearest the horse's tail) in a forward motion.

Different horses may need different combinations of these components or indeed different cues entirely, but this is a good place to start. If it doesn't work, adjust yourself accordingly.

Once you have the horse moving forward, you can easily increase the horse's speed. Two standard ways to do this are:

1) Increasing the energy of the cue.

2) Squeezing the horse harder against the wall.

To increase the energy of your cue put more speed and force into the twisting of your shoulder and hip. To squeeze the horse harder against the wall leave the center of the ring and walk in closer to the horse, focusing your distance increasing signals on his rear end *(see figure 4.5)*. This has the same effect as pushing harder on the bar of soap in the shower.

Actually, there are many horses that do not need your cues focused right on their rear end. All horses have what we call a "balance point." The real truth is that your cues need to be directed behind the balance point, wherever that may be, to get the horse to move forward. Aiming at the rear end is simply a way to be sure that your cues are behind it.

Figure 4.4. The author asking Nelson to move forward.

Figure 4.5. Asking the horse to go forward faster.

The balance point is an imaginary point in space. If our cues are given in the proper relationship to it, they succeed, while if they are not the horse will do something other than what we think we are asking for. We do not know exactly what this balance point is, but we know how the horse reacts to it. When we give distance increasing signals directly at this point, the horse does not move freely forward or backward, but tries to move sideways to get away from us, much like the bar of soap would do if we pressed it exactly in the center. Since the wall prevents this sideways movement, most cooperative horses either show signs of insecurity, try to break down the wall to move away from us, try to escape straight up in the air, or bolt forward to outrun the entire problem *(see figure 3.4)*.

If we project distance increasing signals behind the balance point, a cooperative horse will try to move forward, and if we project them in front of it, the horse will try to move backwards. The balance point is essentially the center of mental balance, but is not the same as the center of gravity or the physical center of balance. The last two exist physically, while the mental balance point we are talking about is imaginary and exists only in the minds of the horse and trainer. It is, however, extremely important for good lungeing.

If you have a horse standing on the wall and you move in until your spaces connect, he will start to move. Whatever direction he moves, take a small step that way until he stops and begins moving the other direction. Then take a small step that way until he stops and again shifts direction. Keep this up until you find a place where you can stand still and make the horse go a little forward and a little back just by leaning right or left. You are now standing directly opposite the balance point. If you are being careful and the horse is only taking slow, relaxed steps to respond, you will notice that the balance point of a stationary or slow moving horse is somewhere from the rear half of the rib cage to the shoulder *(see figure 4.6)*. If you do this with enough horses, you will also notice that it is in a different location for each horse you are working. Don't be alarmed, this is quite normal. There can be great variation between horses, which is one of the things that makes tackless training so interesting. Seldom do you find two horses exactly the same. If you do a great number of horses, you will find some that have different balance points on different sides of their body. With these horses you must direct your cues to different locations depending upon whether they are facing clockwise or counter clockwise.

The balance point not only varies between individuals, but varies in speed in the same horse. More specifically, as the horse moves faster, the balance point moves farther forward on his body until in many cases it will be a point in space out in front of the horse's body. It is not unusual to work horses whose balance points at the canter are out in front of their nose, and some are almost a length in front of the horse *(see figures 4.7, 4.8 and 4.9)*. As the horse slows down, the balance point shifts in the rearward direction until it returns to the original location when the horse stops. In other words, as the horse moves faster, you must direct your cues farther forward for them to be effective.

Returning to the cue for forward movement, you increase the speed of a horse by increasing the energy of your cue or pressing the horse against the wall just behind the balance point; or both. At high speeds you will not be pressing the horse on his rear end, but much farther forward. If you can't determine where the balance point is, it is always safe to press the rear end, which in a fast moving horse is definitely behind the balance point. A horse in a high state of arousal or energy will only need to be asked to increase speed once. Lower energy horses have to be continually pushed to maintain the higher speed.

How you ask a horse to slow down depends upon his energy level. A horse in a low state of arousal (what I call a low energy level) is much like a stalled car being pushed in neutral up a slight hill. As soon as you stop pushing it to go faster, it immediately slows down and soon comes to a stop. So, in free lungeing, all you have to do with a low energy horse is reduce the pressure to go forward and make sure you don't give any high energy cues. The horse will immediately begin slowing down.

The horse with a high energy level is another matter. He wants to keep going forward as quickly as is comfortable, so you can reduce the pressure all you want and he will keep moving forward at the speed he chooses (which is often faster than you would like). With this horse you must project the center of your space in front of the balance point to inhibit forward movement. If this doesn't work, you

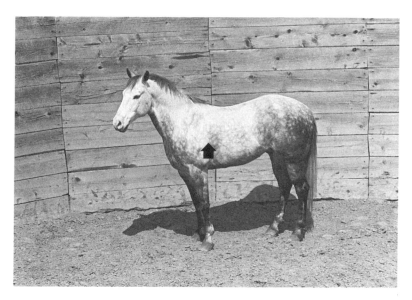

Figure 4.6. The balance point (indicated by the black arrow) of a standing horse can be anywhere from the rear half of the rib cage to the shoulder, depending on the horse.

Figure 4.7. As the horse begins to walk, the balance point moves forward.

Figure 4.8. As the horse increases speed and trots, the balance point moves still farther forward.

Figure 4.9. As the horse increases speed and canters, the balance point moves farther forward, often being out in front of the horse's body.

can try using stronger distance increasing signals ahead of the balance point. Be careful as you do this, or the horse may do an outside turn *(see chapter 5)* and reverse direction. You could also try using the lead hand (nearest the head) as a modifier *(see chapter 12)* to imitate slapping the horse in the chest. If none of these attempts work, you may have to use some outside turns *(see chapter 5)* to focus the horse's attention on you before returning to your attempts to slow him down.

To ask a horse to stop, you essentially need to block his forward movement without giving any signals to go away or come here. The best way to do this is:

1) Project the center of your space in front of the balance point.

2) Step sideways with the lead foot to block any forward motion.

The manner in which you step determines how strong a stop cue you are giving. If you stomp your foot, it will be interpreted as a strong go away signal. The trick to stopping a horse is to give just enough distance increasing signals to have mild pressure on the horse, but not enough to make him turn away from you. So save foot stomping for times when you want to give strong go away signals, such as when the horse is ignoring you. The golden rule of stop cues is that the more weight you place on the front foot, the stronger your cue is. So if you want to give a low intensity cue, keep your weight on the rear foot, the one nearest the tail of the horse, and gently touch the toe of the lead foot, the one nearest the horse's head, to the ground when you step sideways. Cues which have progressively more weight on the lead foot get progressively more severe until you reach the other end of the spectrum with a maximum strength cue having the knee of the lead leg bent with all of your weight on it *(see figures 4.10, 4.11 and 4.12)*. You have to experiment to find which intensity is right for each particular horse at any given time. If you give too strong a cue, the horse will stick his rear end out towards you, or do an outside turn, instead of stopping straight on the wall. Another interesting point to remember is that the faster the horse is moving, the softer the stop cue has to be to keep the horse straight on the wall.

When you step sideways, try to keep your toes pointing straight forward so you can visualize a line drawn from your heel through

Figure 4.10. A weak stop cue. Note the author's weight on his rear leg while he touches just the toe of his lead foot to the ground.

Figure 4.11. A medium strength stop cue with the weight more evenly distributed.

Figure 4.12. A strong stop cue with most of the weight on the lead foot.

your toes straight out in front of you to the round pen wall. Most cooperative horses will stop with their front feet on this imaginary line. Occasionally you will meet horses which line their hind feet up on the line, but they are rare. If a horse goes past this line, you should protest or punish him, whichever is more appropriate for the particular situation.

If the horse ignores your stop cues and consistently goes right through them, you may need to work on outside turns *(see chapter 5)* for a while before you return to the stop cue. With difficult horses we often go right to the outside turn before even attempting a stop. Once the outside turns have focused the horse on the human, the chances of the stop cues working are much higher. An alternative method for stopping a horse is to keep stepping to the side in the direction the horse is traveling until the curvature of the wall brings the horse close enough for your space to pressure the horse into stopping. This will not work on a dominant horse which doesn't respect your space, but it is quite useful with insecure submissive horses which are running because they are temporarily confused. Dominant horses don't need to be helped like this, they need to be whacked when they cross the line you draw with your foot.

Some horses will resist your attempts to stop them straight on the wall. Many of these require multiple, and sometimes conflicting signals with modifiers to get them to stop straight. For instance, some horses will stop for you but will stick their rear end out every time. One approach which has been successful on this type of horse is giving the stop cue with the lead leg and at the same time a go forward cue with the rear hip and shoulder to keep the horse's hips from coming off the wall. Once in a while we even have to add a come here signal (like leaning backwards) on the head to keep it from going away from us towards the wall. So we end up giving stop, go, and come here signals all at the same time in order to obtain a straight stop. Once you have mastered the cues, you will find that there are many interesting combinations. Difficult horses often require such ambivalent mixtures.

The Outside Turn

When reversing the direction of a moving horse, you can turn him either towards the center of the ring or away from it. If you choose the latter and turn the horse away from the center (or inside) towards the wall (or outside), you have turned the horse away from you and performed what is known as an "outside turn" *(see figure 5.1)*. To understand the cues, you simply have to think of what you need to tell the horse. Then consult your list of signals *(see chapter 3)*, select appropriate ones and use them in the correct sequence.

The first thing we need to tell the horse is not to go forward any more. Then we need to tell him to go away from us (towards the wall), then to turn and change direction, and then to go forward again. Any signals we use that accomplish those things in that order should result in an outside turn. While there may be more than one way to accomplish this, we have had good luck with the following sequence:

1) Walk towards the balance point while giving distance increasing signals slightly in front of it.

2) Keep walking until you get a physical reaction from the horse (slowing, leaning, head raising).

3) When you get the reaction, twist your lead shoulder and hip towards the rear of the horse.

4) When the horse has reversed, follow through with your shoulder and hip to cue him forward in the new direction.

Directing your go away signals just in front of the balance point tells the horse not to go forward any more. Continuing these signals

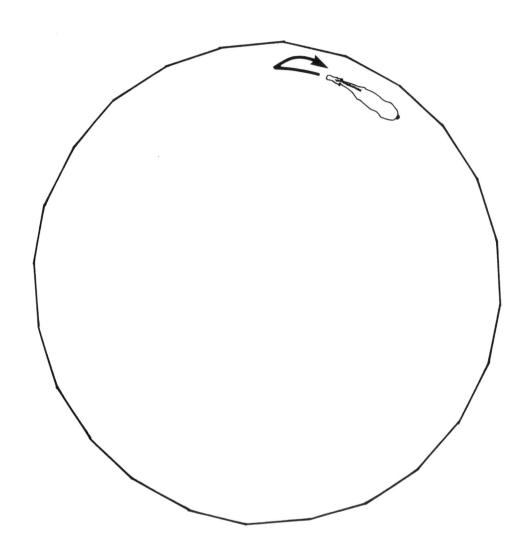

Figure 5.1. The outside turn.

as you move towards the balance point tells the horse to move away from you, but not in the forward direction. Of course, he will be prevented from complying by the wall, which will put the horse under pressure. The physical reaction you see from the horse is a sign that there is enough pressure to make the turn. When you give him the direction by twisting the shoulders and hips, a cooperative horse is more than willing to turn away from the pressure and move out of your space *(see figures 5.1, 5.2, 5.3, 5.4 and 5.5)*. As he does, you should follow through but then allow him to escape from the pressure. Chasing after a cooperative horse does nothing to encourage a cooperative turn the next time you ask for one.

It helps to start learning this maneuver on moving horses, but once you have mastered that, you will find that it can be accomplished just as reliably on horses which are standing still. The balance point is simply in a different place.

There are several common difficulties with this maneuver. One is missing the balance point. If you walk towards the wall behind the balance point, even a cooperative horse will run forward faster to escape the pressure *(see figure 5.6)*. This is quite respectful of the horse since you are asking for it; you are pressing the wet bar of soap against the wall on the rear end and it is squirting out in the forward direction. If you walk towards the wall a little in front of the balance point, the turn should work. However, if you are radically in front of the balance point, the horse is likely to do a turn to the inside, not the outside. This is because the go away signals are so far in front of the horse that there is no pressure actually on the horse to hold him against the wall *(see figure 5.7)*. He is then free to choose which way to turn, as long as he doesn't go forward. If you give the horse that kind of freedom, don't criticize his choices.

Another mistake is walking sideways, parallel with the horse until your space overbalances that of the horse, then twisting the shoulders and getting a good turn from a cooperative horse. This works when the horse wants to cooperate, but does not signal to the horse that you are in charge of the procedure. Dominant horses will turn only when they feel like it (since there is no pressure) and others will have confusion problems.

Figure 5.2. The start of the outside turn. Note the first step is forward towards the wall, not sideways. No reaction yet from the horse.

Figure 5.3. The horse begins to react to the pressure and the author prepares to start the shoulder and hip twist.

Figure 5.4. The horse turns away from the pressure towards the wall and the author begins the directional cue of shoulder twisting.

Figure 5.5. The shoulder and hip twist completes the turn and the horse moves off in the new direction.

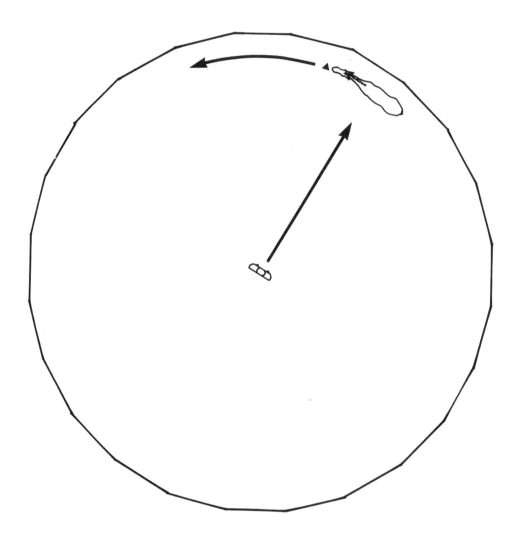

Figure 5.6. Outside turn cues aimed behind the balance point will force the horse to run forward even faster.

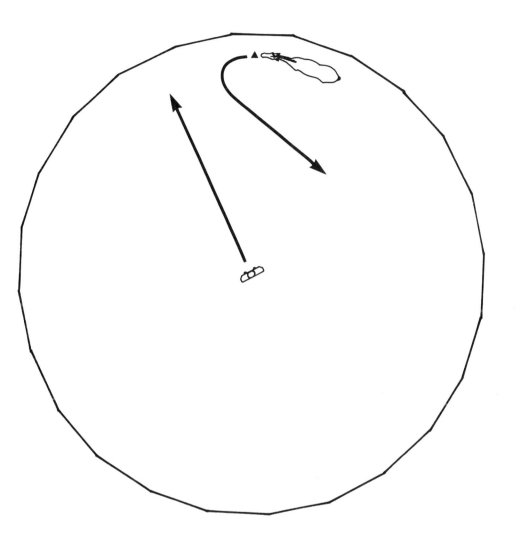

Figure 5.7. Outside turn cues aimed too far in front of the balance point often result in an inside turn instead.

The confusion comes from the fact that in order to walk sideways, you must take your first step in that direction. When you do, you have given a stop cue *(see chapter 4)*.

As horses gain experience, they begin to read your first step and anticipate which cue is coming, so when you step sideways they stop, and when you take an energetic step towards them or their balance point, they begin an outside turn. This allows you to remain in the center of the ring with the horse doing all the work. If, however, both your stop and outside turn cues start with a sideways step, you will never reach this stage. Some horses will do stops when you want an outside turn, some will do outside turns when you ask for a stop and some will get so annoyed with you that they will just resist you on everything. So try to make your signals distinct and separate. If you want a stop, step sideways; if you want an outside turn, step and move towards the horse or his balance point *(see figures 5.8 and 5.9)*. If you don't make this clear distinction, you will pay for it later.

Another problem is twisting the shoulders before the horse has reacted physically. Some people get it in their head that you take a certain number of steps and twist the shoulders, regardless. However, if there is not sufficient pressure on the horse when you twist the shoulders, all but the most cooperative will run right through your cue. The shoulders do not make the horse turn. Pressure against the wall makes the horse turn. Without pressure, the horse may choose whether to turn or not. They don't always make decisions you will like. To avoid this, make sure you hold the shoulder and hip twist until you see a physical reaction indicating that the horse feels pressure. Keep walking towards the balance point until you see this reaction.

This pressure can be used to mold the mind of the horse. If the horse is dominant, or for some other reason resisting you out of confidence, the outside turn pressures him into yielding to you. With enough repetitions, the horse will either begin to think of you as a superior or start competing with you for leadership. If he competes, repeating enough outside turns will eventually convince him that you are indeed the leader. So you will either solve your problem or bring it to a head and then solve it *(see chapter 9)*. The outside turn is a valuable tool for working with dominant horses.

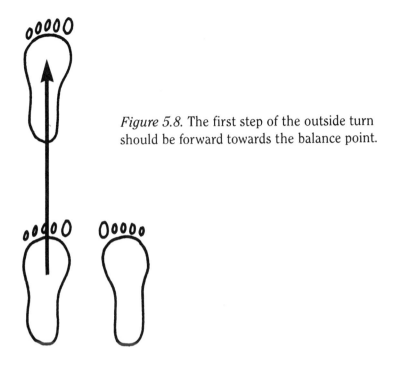

Figure 5.8. The first step of the outside turn should be forward towards the balance point.

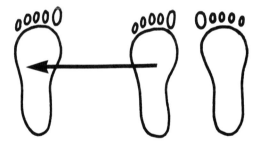

Figure 5.9. A common mistake is to move sideways when asking for an outside turn. This is a stop cue, not a turn cue.

For the same reasons, the outside turn can be overused on submissive or insecure horses. If the horse is already submissive and you use a lot of outside turns with pressure, he will begin to react in an overly submissive manner towards you. If he is insecure, he will become more frightened of you the more pressure you subject him to. In other words, using too many outside turns with pressure on submissive or insecure horses will create problems. However, you don't have to avoid the outside turn completely. Fortunately, there is a way to ask the horse for the outside turn without putting undue amounts of pressure on him. You essentially have to do what you were just told not to do with the dominant horse, cue for the turn without getting in close enough to create pressure. If the horse is truly submissive or insecure, the turn will be perfect and the horse's body language will show more confident indicators than when you use turns with pressure. The next thing you can do is to start stepping backwards with your feet as soon as the horse commits himself to the turn. In other words, you step in towards the balance point until the horse begins to turn and then you immediately start stepping backwards as you twist your shoulders and hips for the turn. This releases any small amounts of pressure that may have been felt by the horse and serves to lower tension levels, even in confident horses. This releasing outside turn is also quite valuable for working horses whose energy levels are higher than you would like. If you turn them hard and then back away they will begin to lower their energy levels after several turns and most become more manageable.

So, how you do the outside turn depends on the confidence level of the horse involved. If he is a confident horse, you move in and pressure him against the wall. If he lacks confidence, you ease up on your distance increasing signals and turn the horse without much pressure. Using a weak turn on a confident horse will portray you as a weak leader, causing you trouble later. Using too strong a turn on insecure horses will scare them, making your problem worse. If you can't tell which type of horse you are dealing with, try a normal turn with pressure, read the horse as he reacts to you and adjust accordingly. If you can't read the horse, you don't need to learn tackless training yet, you need to learn how to read horses — and that is beyond the scope of this book.

CHAPTER 6

The Inside Turn

Another way to encourage a moving horse to reverse direction is to have him turn towards you in the center of the ring, or away from the wall. By having the horse turn in towards you like this, you are doing what is known as an "inside turn" *(see figure 6.1)*. To accomplish this we once again need to consider what we need to tell the horse, consult our list of available signals in chapter 3 and act accordingly. Essentially, we need to tell the horse to come towards us away from the wall and towards the center of the ring, to turn far enough to reverse direction and then to continue forward in the new direction. Any signals which accomplish this should be successful but I suggest you use the following sequence as a starting point:

1) Break eye contact by turning your head to look at the space behind the horse. Some people like to think of this as looking in the direction of the horse's tail, others prefer to state it as looking in the direction they would like the horse to go when the maneuver is completed. Use whichever phrase makes most sense to you.

2) Stand up straight, lean back and walk backwards away from the horse extending your lead arm as you do so (the lead arm is the one nearest the horse's head). This will be the left arm when the horse is moving counter clockwise and the right arm when he is moving clockwise. Some horses perform better if you have the whip in the lead hand as you do this. Your lead arm, whip and shoulder should be pointing towards the wall in front of the balance point, not at the horse.

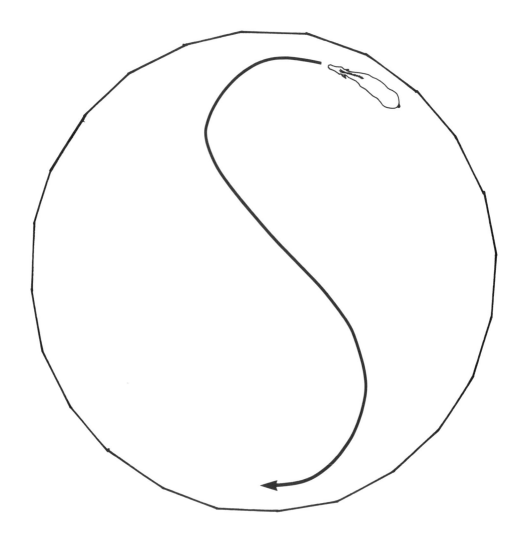

Figure 6.1. The inside turn.

3) As the horse comes off the wall towards you and the midline of his body turns far enough to pass your position, push him around by twisting your lead shoulder and cue the horse to move away from you in the new direction.

4) If the horse does not come off the wall, keep moving backwards until you feel the wall of the training pen at your back, maintain your signals and wait for the horse to come to you there. If your head, arm and shoulder are angled properly you should be able to peel the horse off the wall.

Breaking eye contact, leaning back and walking back away from the horse all invite him to come your direction. As the body axis of the horse (or his spine) turns far enough to pass your position, you essentially switch from distance decreasing to distance increasing signals and drive him away from you back to the wall and forward in the new direction *(see figures 6.2, 6.3, 6.4, and 6.5)*

Horses are often sensitive to the angle at which you walk away from them in step 2. I have come to call this your "angle of departure." It needs to be adjusted according to how fast the horse is moving. When the horse is moving at a fast walk or slow trot, it is best to move straight away at a 90 degree angle from the horses body axis *(see figure 6.6)*.

As the speed of the horse changes from this slow trot, there is a rule of thumb you can follow. In general, the slower the horse is moving the more you should angle towards his head *(see figure 6.7)* and the faster he is moving the more you should angle back towards the tail end of the horse *(see figure 6.8)*. If you do not do this, you will lose your space connection with the slower horses and many of them will slow to a stop and stand still. The faster ones will throw their heads out towards the wall and do an outside turn because you have put too much pressure on their front end. So when you are not getting the inside turn the way you would like it, you would be wise to change your angle of departure and see what happens. Many times it is the answer to your problems.

If you reach step 4 and find yourself standing with your back to the wall and a stationary horse opposite you, there is another option. You can maintain your signals while slowly walking sideways around the

Figure 6.2. The beginning of the inside turn. The author has broken eye contact, is leaning and walking backwards and is starting to extend the lead arm.

Figure 6.3. As the distance decreasing signals continue, the horse starts to turn to the inside.

Figure 6.4. The horse moves farther around to the inside.

Figure 6.5. As the horse completes the turn, the author prepares to step forward and ask him to keep going forward.

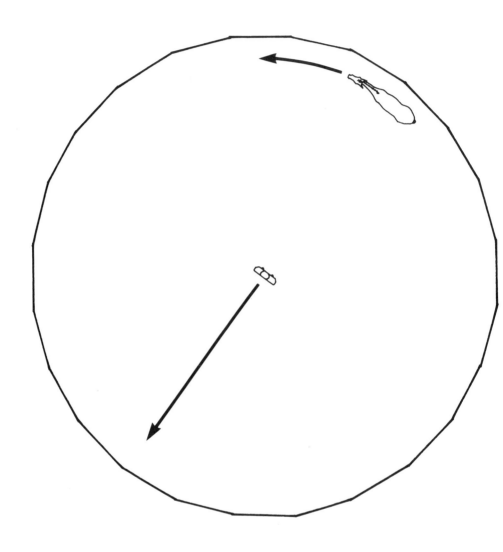

Figure 6.6. The standard angle of departure for the inside turn.

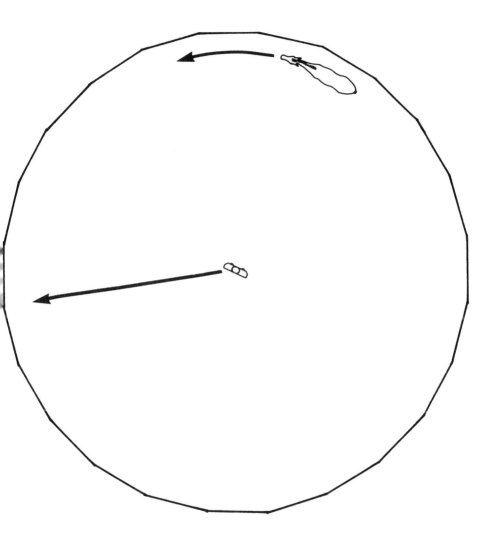

Figure 6.7. With a very slow moving horse or one that loses impulsion, you need to angle more towards the head to maintain contact.

wall towards the horse *(see figure 6.9)*. If his head turns out towards the wall, stop for a moment. When the head comes back in away from the wall, continue moving. In this way you can sometimes encourage a motionless horse to turn inwards and complete the turn properly.

Some people are in too much of a hurry to move backwards away from the horse. When they are in this frame of mind they often switch the whip over to the lead hand with force and energy. Fast movements of the hands, especially when there is a whip involved, are, of course, distance increasing signals and the horse will often feel pressure on the front end and do an outside turn. Other people will plant one foot and lean forward at the waist in order to push off hard and propel themselves backwards. If this is done quickly, what they have actually done is to stamp one foot while they lean forwards towards the horse. By the time they move backwards it is too late, since the horse has already seen two distance increasing signals — foot stamping and leaning forward — and will usually move away from them and do an outside turn. It is important to switch the whip slowly and ahead of time and to stand up straight and lean backwards with the top of the body in step 2 before walking backwards away from the horse.

As mentioned in chapter 5, you can get an inside turn accidentally by aiming your signals for an outside turn too far ahead of the balance point. However, I have not been able to do this deliberately when I want an inside turn. For some reason when I am trying to get an inside turn that way, the horse always turns to the outside. Perhaps you will have more luck than I have had with this. If you do, please let me know how you do it.

Since the inside turn does not rely on pressure, it is a good maneuver to use when working insecure horses *(see chapter 10)*. If you use it too much on dominant horses, they may think less of you, but it is not a problem when used in moderation. Some trainers prefer it to the outside turn for race horses so that they do not learn to duck into the rail when they feel pressure from the other side.

One other point is worth mentioning. Many people have more difficulty learning the inside turn than the outside turn. Perhaps this is because they cannot use pressure to make the horse do it. At any rate, don't despair if you come along slowly with this maneuver. It may require a little more work, but with good coaching you will master it.

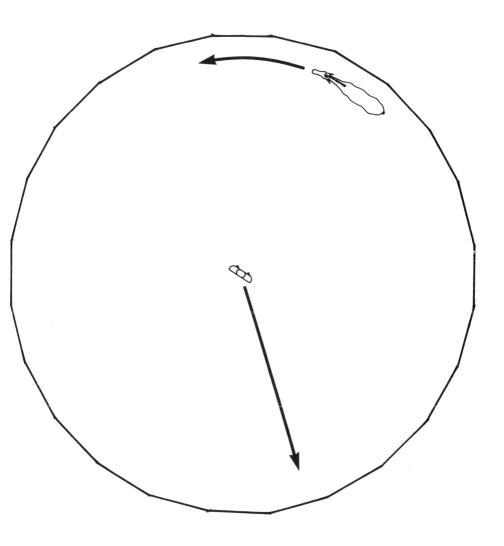

Figure 6.8. With a fast or energetic horse you need to angle back more towards his hips to avoid pushing his head outwards towards the wall.

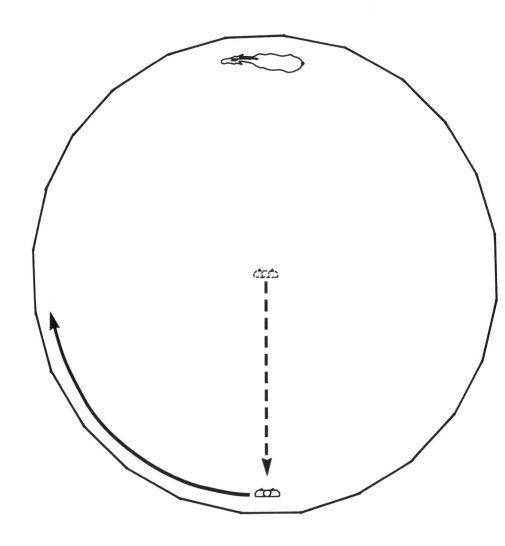

Figure 6.9. How to approach a horse that doesn't come off the wall.

CHAPTER 7

Backing up

When a horse is standing still on the wall, it is possible to ask him to walk backwards. It is not wise to continue this for too long, since it is physically difficult for horses to move in this direction, but it is not a difficult maneuver to accomplish. Again, we simply think of what we need to tell the horse, consult our list of signals in chapter 3 and speak to him accordingly.

What we need to tell the horse is to stay against the wall without turning and to move in the rearward direction. Any signals that accomplish this are acceptable, but consider the following as a starting point:

1) Make sure that the horse is standing next to the wall such that there is no space between him and the barrier.

2) Be certain you are standing opposite the balance point or a few inches in front of it.

3) Make sure your personal spaces are connected.

4) Raise the rear hand and extend it towards the horse's hip to pressure him to stay in against the wall. The rear hand is the one nearest the tail. This will be the right hand when the horse is facing counter clockwise and the left hand when he is facing clockwise.

5) With the whip in the lead hand, swing the lead arm from the front in a rearwards direction towards the horse's chest, to pressure him to move away. Keep the arm straight and don't twist the shoulders too much (that would be a turn cue).

69

The hips can also be effective in this situation. If there is no response, move a step closer to the horse and repeat your signals. Keep doing this until the horse begins to move in the rearward direction. With many horses it is wise to protest between signals if they don't move by waving the whip in the air or hitting the ground with it. The sequence would then be signal, protest, step closer, repeat the signal. If it doesn't work, again protest, step closer and repeat. Be careful, since protesting may frighten timid horses. Stop pressing when the horse has moved far enough to the rear.

What we have done here is to use distance increasing signals to put pressure on the side and front of the horse *(see figures 7.1 and 7.2)*. Since the wall is restricting him to the outside, the path of least resistance is backwards *(see figure 7.3)*. Effectively, we have pressed the bar of soap against the wall on its front end and it is squeezing out to the rear.

A common problem with this maneuver is the horse bolts forward instead of moving backwards. This usually is a sign that you were behind the balance point when you began your signals *(see figure 7.4)*. Remember that you are in effect giving distance increasing signals and that the center of your space is a powerful directional cue. If you have focused behind the balance point and are telling the horse to move away, the most respectful thing for him to do is to bolt forward to get out of your space as quickly as possible.

Another problem commonly encountered is that of having the horse do an outside turn instead of walking backwards. This usually happens when you have left too much space between the horse and the wall, allowing him the freedom to turn in such a manner *(see figure 7.5)*. Moving the horse out flush against the wall before beginning the maneuver will solve this problem.

Occasionally, however, the horse will begin moving backwards and then do an outside turn even though you have him flush against the wall. Sometimes this is due to your using too much shoulder, making your signal look like that of an outside turn cue. More often it is a sign that you have put more pressure in front of the balance point than you have behind it. Submissive horses will try to accommodate you and dominant horses will use it as an excuse to evade you. In either case, if you decrease pressure on the front end of the horse and

Figure 7.1. Asking the horse to walk backwards. Note the pressure on the horse's hip from the rear hand while the lead arm sweeps towards the horse from in front of the chest.

Figure 7.2. Completing the backup.

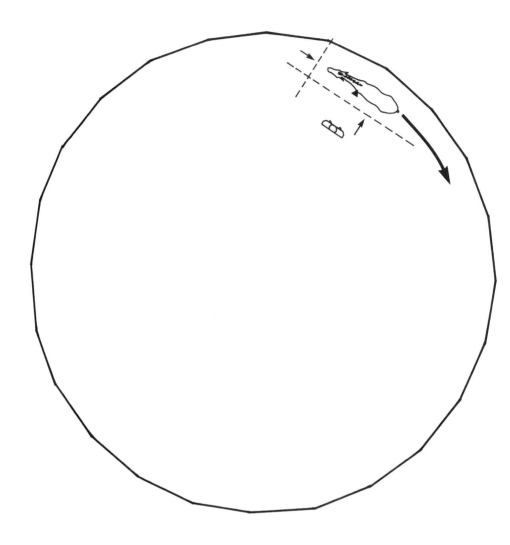

Figure 7.3. The backup showing the unseen forces involved and the balance point (the black triangle).

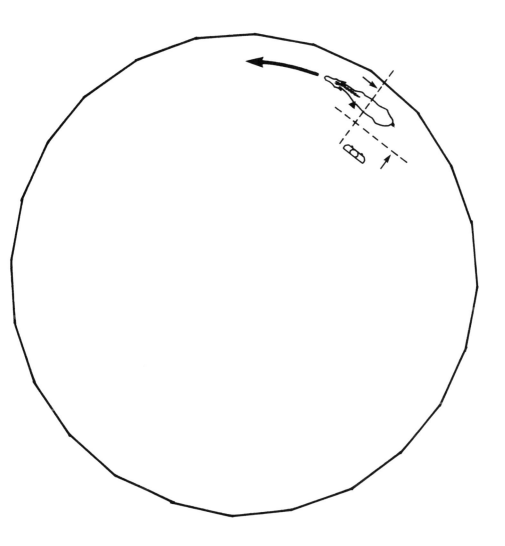

Figure 7.4. What happens when you project your signals behind the balance point.

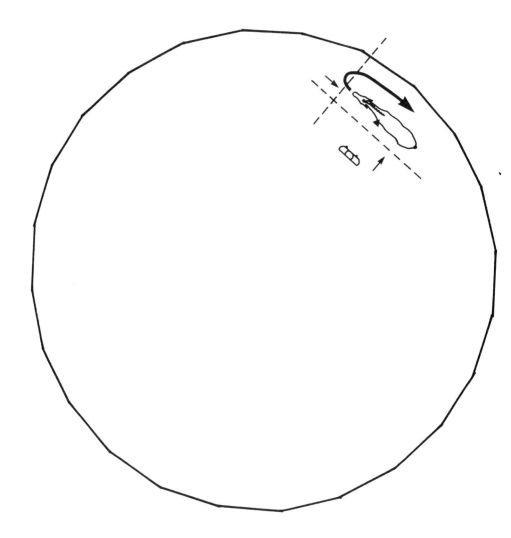

Figure 7.5. What can happen if you leave too much room between the horse and the wall before asking for the backup.

increase pressure on the rear end to a point where they match each other properly, the horse will move backwards in the correct manner. Sometimes this involves less movement of the lead arm, sometimes pushing against the horse's hip with the rear hand more forcefully (by bending the elbow and shoving out violently towards his hip) and still others will involve both.

As you concentrate on manipulating the horse's movements, it is not unusual to find that you have crept in too close with your feet. When this happens, you will notice that your horse becomes more frantic and overly reactive. A good rule of thumb for all maneuvers in tackless training is that if you see a frantic or overly reactive horse in front of you, keep signaling while your feet take a step backwards away from him. This will often reduce pressure enough to allow the horse to behave better. Most of us are still convinced that in order to have control, we must have a physical connection to the horse and we must be close to him. This is not true, of course, but many people find that their natural reaction is to creep closer when things are not going their way. This is fine if the problem is that your personal spaces haven't connected yet, but once the connection is made, try to remember that movement towards the horse is a distance increasing signal which will pressure him if you have him trapped against the wall.

CHAPTER 8

Calling Your Horse to You

The preceding chapters have discussed maneuvers which involve combinations of signals from different categories in order to control direction and movement. What do you suppose would happen if we gave as many signals as possible from a single category, namely distance decreasing? There should be a strong desire on the part of the horse to walk right over to us, providing he respects us, is not afraid of us, and our spaces are well connected. This calling of the horse over to us is often used to end the workout, to give a reward after a particularly good performance, to defuse tension between the trainer and a confident horse, or to boost the confidence of a timid horse by inviting him into the herd leader's space. Whatever the use, it is often referred to as the "come in" or the "call in" since you are usually asking the horse to come into the center of the ring *(see figure 8.1)*.

It is best attempted when the horse is standing still, but I have seen it succeed on slowly moving horses as well. While any number of combinations should work, we have had good luck with the following sequence of signals:

1) Signal the moving horse to stop by stepping sideways with your lead foot as described in chapter 4. Leave the lead foot in place to tell the horse not to go forward while you are signaling him.

2) Step back away from the horse with the rear foot and turn the top of your body about 45 degrees away from the horse. Do not twist so far that your lead shoulder points towards the horse. Only 45 degrees, not 90.

77

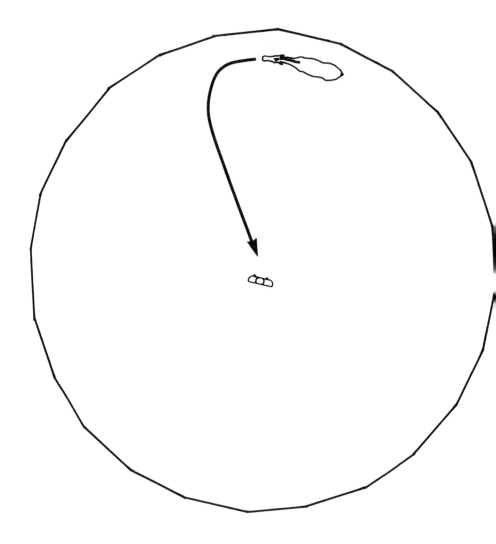

Figure 8.1. The call in.

3) Break eye contact and lean back away from the horse as far as you can without hurting yourself.

4) A gentle, slow, drawing in motion of the hand will often encourage the horse to approach you. It is not necessary for many horses and some actually dislike it. If you use it, remember to be slow and gentle — fast hand movements are go away signals.

5) Hold this position until the horse comes over to you or gives the appearance of not being interested *(see figures 8.2, 8.3, 8.4, 8.5 and 8.6).*

If the horse starts to walk forward on the wall, repeat your stop cue and call him in again. If he is a timid horse he will be afraid to enter your space so be sure to give him plenty of time and several cues before you give up.

Should the horse show no interest, there are a few things you can try. Sometimes the connection between your spaces needs to be stronger. So, walk slowly towards the horse until you get some physical reaction such as a muscle twitch or head raise or body lean that indicates that the horse feels your presence in his space. Then repeat the come in cue; often the horse will walk over to you.

If this doesn't work, increase the strength of your distance decreasing signals. This can be done by approaching the horse until you get one of the reactions described above. Then repeat the come in cue except that, instead of just leaning back, walk backwards away from the horse quickly to pull hard on the connection between your spaces *(see figure 8.7).* The trick is to repeat this maneuver several times, walking in slowly and backing out quickly to "suck him off the wall" as we like to say. If you get even a small step away from the wall on the part of the horse, it is sometimes enough. Approach the horse quietly without giving any go away signals, lead him to the center and reward him. Then either end the workout or continue with something else as seems appropriate.

With more repetitions, the come in will get better and better. Some people who have not learned how to make their space small enough actually have to get down on one knee and drop their eyes to the ground before horses will consider coming in to them. If you do this,

Figure 8.2. Beginning the come in cue. Note the lead foot is left in place after the stop cue while all other cues are distance decreasing. The hand is slowly motioning in the author's direction.

Figure 8.3. The horse begins to move towards the center of the ring.

Figure 8.4. He continues to approach the distance decreasing signals.

Figure 8.5. The horse arrives at the center of the ring.

Figure 8.6. The horse receives positive reinforcement in the form of mutual grooming.

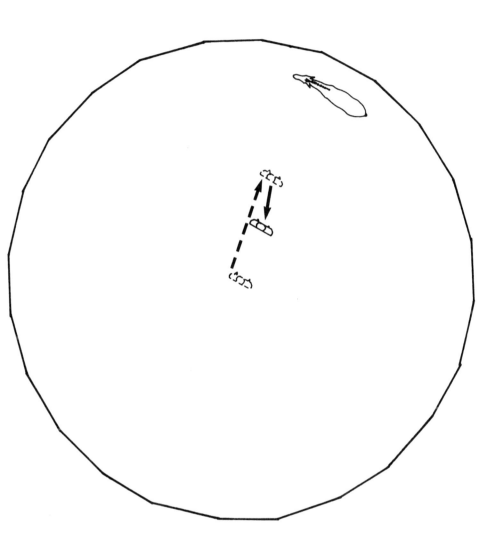

Figure 8.7. Some horses need to be approached slowly and backed away from quickly to pull them off the wall.

be careful to keep an eye on the horse out of the corner of your eye and only put one knee on the ground. It is unsafe to take your eyes completely off the horse or kneel down on both knees.

I used to think that I had to make every horse come in to me as soon as possible but I no longer feel that way. If a horse is not interested in coming in to me, I simply wait until our relationship gets better. With good free lungeing it is only a matter of time before they start wanting to come in, so I just wait for them to get motivated. Until that time, however, I make a mental note that the horse is holding something back from me.

CHAPTER 9

Submission Training

Once you have learned all the physical maneuvers involved in this style of tackless training, you have only seen the tip of the iceberg. You must now learn how to put all these maneuvers together to affect the manner in which the horse thinks. Otherwise, all you have done is given the horse physical exercise, and that is not the best use of tackless training.

It is true that some horses come into the training pen ready to work for you with no problems. These horses are a joy to work with and should be treasured. Make sure that you recognize such horses quickly so that you don't start trying to change the way they think. If it's not broken, don't fix it. Just give these horses a chance to work for a good leader and let them live happy lives. Don't go looking for trouble where there isn't any.

On the other hand, some horses come into the training pen with a superior attitude. They feel dominant over the human trainer and resist our cues with very confident body language. Some are aggressive in their resistance, others are not, but they all display extreme confidence. What we need to do with these horses is to train them in such a way that they begin to think in a more submissive manner when working with us. When they do, they will be much easier to work with and safer as well. Such training has come to be called "submission training" by behaviorists and trainers alike. It should never be used on timid, frightened, or overly submissive horses, only dominant ones.

What it consists of is setting up your training system to do exactly the opposite of what the horse wants to do at any given moment. In short, you read the horse to see what he wants to do, and you choose to work on what he does not want to work on in a way he doesn't want to do it, at a time he would rather be doing something else. You don't expect the horse to be good at anything when you work this way, but you keep it up until he does something you can consider slightly cooperative. You then either end the workout or change things to suit the horse more.

With time the horse learns that the way to stop all this irritation is to give you what you want (cooperation), at least temporarily. With more time he learns that life is just plain better being cooperative and that you are a good leader anyway. The great majority of them will then give you the leadership role willingly and start thinking more submissively towards you. You get a major change in their thought process but without a big physical confrontation. In the end you are more likely to win with this approach and there is much less chance of physical injury to both you and the horse. It is not faster than starting a big fight and winning, but there is no chance of losing the big fight either. When done properly, you are guaranteed to win and it is safer for both parties. Regardless of whether you are using tackless training or not, select a time of day when the horse will not want to work. Sometimes this is a favorite nap time or perhaps 30 minutes before regular feeding time. As soon as you get some type of cooperation the horse can return to his nap or get fed (provided he is cooled out), as the case may be. Then pay attention to whether the horse wants company today or not. If he seems to want to be with other horses today, make sure there are no other horses around the training area. If he is an aloof horse, make sure there are other horses around the area when he works. In general, make sure that the training environment is exactly what the horse does not want. When he shows you the least bit of cooperation, he can have all these things, but not until.

When the horse arrives at the training pen, pay attention to his energy level, or arousal state. If he is full of energy and wants to move quickly, you choose to work on slow walks, stops and walking backwards. If the energy level is low, you choose to warm him up into a faster workout emphasizing high energy maneuvers. He will not be good at any of these things, but sooner or later he will attempt to cooperate. That is when you stop the workout and give him what he wants.

It is usually a mistake to work a horse longer than his attention span. However, if the horse is dominant and still resisting you, it can be quite useful to work him so long that he fatigues mentally. He will then be more likely to yield to you without a big fight. Consequently, I often add this to the manipulations listed above as part of submission training. While severe dominance cases need this type of environmental manipulation, many dominant horses will change their thinking without it. They will respond well to regular training sessions that emphasize maneuvers which pressure them mentally. Such maneuvers would include the outside turn, the stop and the back.

Adjusting to the energy level of the horse will complete the process. For example, if the horse has a lot of energy today, you pressure him by matching his energy level for a few minutes and then bringing him down, working on slow walks, stops and walking backwards. If he has little energy today, you match the low energy for a few minutes and then warm him up until you can work at the fast trot and canter with lots of fast outside turns. Essentially, anything that forces the horse to change his energy level and squeezes him against the wall will encourage a dominant horse to think more submissively towards you. Just be careful not to pressure him so much that you start a big fight. It is much safer to chip away at his dominance one little piece at a time. Some people, of course, enjoy starting big fights and feel macho when they win them. This does work, but it is not a compliment to their training skills.

One trap to watch out for is maintaining submission training too long. If you use it correctly, the horse will begin behaving like a more submissive horse. At this point it is very important that you change your technique and treat him like a normal horse. If you continue submission training on a horse that is already submitting, you advertise yourself as a poor leader. You will drive the horse into the overly submissive category, which is just another kind of problem. Base your decisions on what the horse is like now, not what he was like ten minutes ago.

CHAPTER 10

Confidence Building

I n the last chapter we noted that some horses think too dominantly and need to be trained in a particular manner. While this is true, it is also true that many horses have the opposite problem: they think too submissively to be useful. Many are naturally fearful due to their genetic makeup; some have been handled too harshly by humans or other horses; and some have been accidentally subjected to trauma. Regardless of how they became timid, they all need more confidence in order to have happy, productive lives. Tackless training is a wonderful tool for this task.

Manipulating the environment is again important for severe cases, but now we try to set it up so that the horse is comfortable with his surroundings. Then we estimate what the horse will likely do anyway and tell him to do exactly that. When he complies, we give large rewards and repeat the process. Eventually the horse learns that he can succeed when you are the leader and he will begin to feel more confident about life — at least when you are around. Later he will make the transition to other trainers, and eventually to all humans.

The trick is to never ask him to do anything he won't do readily for you, unless you can physically help him through the task without frightening him. This is a form of what psychologists call "shaping," so no punishments are given. If the horse fails to comply, the trainer recognizes that he made a mistake in asking for that maneuver and either helps the horse through it or ignores the disobedience completely.

This is a low stress way to train and a wonderful way to build the confidence of a fearful horse. He soon learns that he now has a good leader he can trust, that there are no punishments or painful events to fear, and that work is easy and always something he can succeed at. He begins to think and act more confidently.

As the horse develops, the maneuvers you choose and the speed at which you work can either help or hinder him. If you emphasize the maneuvers which squeeze him against the wall as we did in the last chapter with the dominant horse, you will frighten him, making the problem worse. If you keep asking the horse to change energy levels, he will eventually fail at something. Instead, keep your workout at the energy level the horse seems comfortable with. While you are doing this, you select maneuvers that release pressure, such as the inside turn and the call in. If all the horse can do is stand there, use your stop cue to tell him to stop and stand (which he is already doing). Call him in and reward him.

Use slow starts and, when you have to stop the horse, use the softest, lightest stop cue that will work and immediately call the horse in to you. The more you call the horse in and reward him, the quicker he will improve. However, many horses are afraid to come into your space even when they think they are being asked, so be ready to help them at first. If the horse is so frightened or tense that he is driven into a high energy state where he can't stop or even move slowly, tell him to go forward at the speed at which you think he wants to move and use inside turns to reverse him. If you have to use outside turns, use them sparingly. As the energy expends itself, the horse may be more comfortable at a slower speed. When you see that he is going to slow down by himself, tell him to slow down and start stopping and calling him in.

With time you may run into the big trap of confidence building. That is, if you do your job correctly, the horse will become so confident that he will be tempted to think dominantly, and some will actually do it. If your poor underdog starts acting in a dominant manner, congratulate yourself for doing a good job but make sure he gets the appropriate punishment. This is often difficult when you have spent so much time avoiding punishments, but it is very important. Remember that confidence building often creates a brat, and brats need to be punished, at least once. Fortunately, once is all it takes in many instances, and the horse settles into a normal life with you as the leader but free of his former fears. The thing to remember is that when the horse acts in a confident manner, treat him like a confident horse. Adapt your treatment to the way the horse is acting now, not the way he was yesterday or last month.

CHAPTER 11

Priorities

M any horses will perform all the maneuvers described in the preceding chapters the first time you attempt them, but this is not always the case. Some horses comply with some maneuvers and resist others while some horses hardly do anything for you at all.

When I first began tackless training, I felt that I had to get the horse to do all the maneuvers as quickly as possible. It was sort of a personal thing, probably linked to some form of ego or machismo. This naturally provoked a good number of fights in the training pen with resistant horses and frightened a good number of timid ones.

As time passed and I became more experienced with the new style, my thinking began to change. I discovered that it was much safer for my students to chip away at a dominant horse slowly without actually starting a fight *(see chapter 9)* and that the final result was just as good, if not better. The horses accepted us as leader just as well as when we started fights and their performance levels were top notch. If the dominance training was weaved into regular workouts, there was no training time lost and it was much safer for the horse as well. With insecure horses I found that if we left out the maneuvers they were afraid of and concentrated on building their confidence first, we saved a lot of training time and got a much better final result.

All this is a long way of saying that it is not always good to insist on complete compliance immediately when training horses. Some come along better if you leave some maneuvers out initially and work later on the things they find difficult or offensive. Which brings us to the question of which maneuvers to start with and what kind of priorities to follow as you progress.

Let us consider the extremely dominant horse. The first priority when you begin working such a horse is that he stay out of your space when you are giving distance increasing signals. This preserves your physical safety and sends the message that you are a high ranking animal also. If you get nothing else accomplished in the first session or two, that is all right. Persevere on that one item until you accomplish it without a blood bath.

Next try to turn the horse as he moves so that you can control his direction in a crude sort of way. Don't tell a real dominant horse how fast to turn, or which direction *(inside or outside, see chapters 5 and 6)*. Just tell him to turn to the outside and if he does, leave him alone. We don't care if he turns inside or outside, fast or slow, in or out of balance. We don't care if he comes out of the turn with good impulsion or even if he is under control. We only care that he changed direction in response to our pressure. If we accomplish that, we back off and show him some respect. At this point we are compromising; if the horse will show us some respect, we will show him some in return.

However, with each passing moment we are asking for just a bit more from him until he either starts working for us or objects to our behavior. If he objects, we back off to a point where he doesn't, and either continue working there for today or end the workout. Each day we ask for a little more, and soon we are demanding good turns, under control. Then we move to stops and backs. Each time the horse objects, we back off slightly and start the process all over again. Soon we are in control and there was no chance of physical injury to either horse or human. So with a dominant horse your priorities, in order of importance, would be:

1) Stay out of my space unless you are invited.

2) Turn in some fashion when I tell you to.

3) Turn properly when I tell you to.

4) Do things at the speed I tell you to work at.

5) Stop and walk backwards when I tell you to.

The timid, insecure or frightened horse is a bit different. Your main concern with this horse is not to frighten him and to give him a feeling of herd acceptance and security. So when we start working him, we minimize distance increasing signals whenever possible and make them weak when we have to use them. We call the horse in to the center of the ring as frequently as we can.

Many frightened horses will be reluctant to do this. You may have to signal first *(see chapter 8),* and then gently approach the horse and lead him into the center, and socialize with him for a while before sending him gently back out to the wall. After a while he will begin to feel accepted by you and less afraid. Do not ask him to do something at which he will fail unless you can help him through it. With some timid horses we literally ask for only three or four steps forward, call them in, and then send them back out to the wall, then ask for another three steps and call them back in. We repeat this all the way around the training arena for the entire fifteen minute session or until the horse starts acting confidently enough to attempt an inside turn or something else. Outside turns are left for later when the horse gets better *(see chapter 10).* So your priorities for an insecure horse, in order of importance, would be:

1) Minimize the use and severity of distance increasing signals.

2) Call the horse in and reward him as frequently as possible.

3) Only ask for things the horse can do well.

By following the proper priorities, you will be successful with a larger number of horses, they will work under less stress, and both you and the horse will be safer. They are worth paying attention to.

CHAPTER 12

Beyond the Basics

T he information in the preceding chapters is designed to get you started in tackless training, but it is not the whole story. Beyond the basic maneuvers are a series of modifiers that can be used to back up the major signals. For instance, it is sometimes helpful to extend the lead arm to slow a horse down by pretending to slap the horse in the chest from the front with the open palm of your hand. Many times the horse will keep moving forward but slow to a more manageable speed when you do this. When you get good, you can use your shoulder, hip and sometimes your knee to obtain the same effect. These maneuvers should not be attempted by beginners, but as you get more experience they can add great depth to your abilities.

Sometimes you can accomplish more with a horse by increasing the restrictions you place on him. This can be done by putting him in a mental vice by moving close to him and extending both arms, one from the front and one from the rear of the horse to push him forward and backward at the same time. This crushes the body of the horse, forcing him to collect himself and move his knees higher. This really gets a horses attention and works wonders on a distractable horse. By putting more pressure on the front of the horse, you can also encourage him to shift weight off the forehand and work in better physical balance. If you overdo it, however, the horse will rear or attempt some other form of escape.

You will find other ways to use modifiers, but resist the temptation to do so before you have mastered the basics. If you try to run before you can walk, you will not only cheat yourself, but your horses as well.